PIANO • VOCAL • GUITAR

BROADWAY TODAY

W9-AFW-349

Cover photo by Anne Clausen

ISBN 0-634-06797-4

HAL•LEONARD®
CORPORATION
7777 W. BLUEMOUND RD. P.O. BOX 13819 MILWAUKEE, WI 53213

Visit Hal Leonard Online at
www.halleonard.com

ELABORATE LIVES

from Walt Disney Theatrical Productions' AIDA

Music by ELTON JOHN
Lyrics by TIM RICE

Moderately, with rubato

EVERY STORY IS A LOVE STORY

from Walt Disney Theatrical Productions' AIDA

Music by ELTON JOHN
Lyrics by TIM RICE

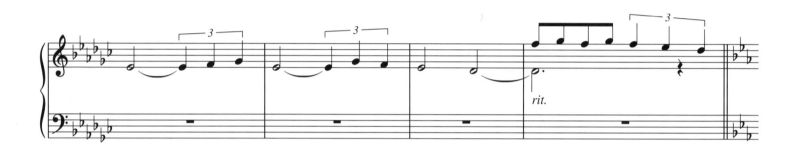

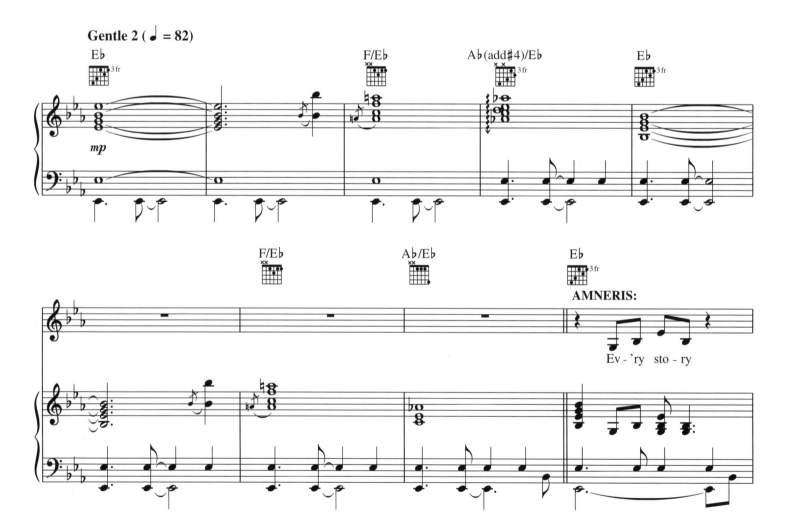

Ev - 'ry sto - ry

AMNERIS:

WRITTEN IN THE STARS

from Walt Disney Theatrical Productions' AIDA

Music by ELTON JOHN
Lyrics by TIM RICE

GASTON

from Walt Disney's BEAUTY AND THE BEAST: THE BROADWAY MUSICAL

Lyrics by HOWARD ASHMAN
Music by ALAN MENKEN

IF I CAN'T LOVE HER

from Walt Disney's BEAUTY AND THE BEAST: THE BROADWAY MUSICAL

Music by ALAN MENKEN
Lyrics by TIM RICE

A CHANGE IN ME

from Walt Disney's BEAUTY AND THE BEAST: THE BROADWAY MUSICAL

Words by TIM RICE
Music by ALAN MENKEN

CABARET

from the Musical CABARET

Words by FRED EBB
Music by JOHN KANDER

DON'T CRY OUT LOUD
(We Don't Cry Out Loud)
from THE BOY FROM OZ

Words and Music by PETER ALLEN
and CAROLE BAYER SAGER

Don't cry ___ out loud, _____ just keep it in - side, learn how to
Fly high ___ and proud, _____ and if you should fall re - mem - ber you

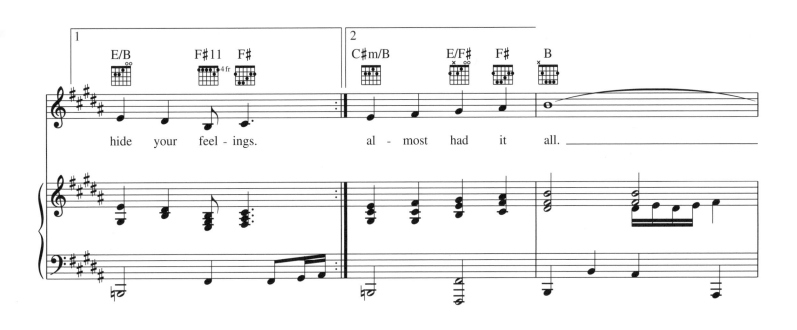

hide your feel - ings. al - most had it all. _____

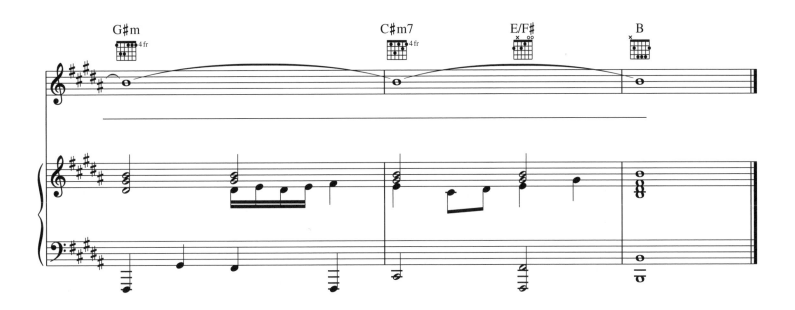

I GO TO RIO

from THE BOY FROM OZ

Words and Music by PETER ALLEN
and ADRIENNE ANDERSON

Vocal ad lib

When my baby
When my baby smiles at me
I go to Rio de Janeiro
It's when I go to Rio
Rio de Janeiro

MAYBE THIS TIME

from the Musical CABARET

Words by FRED EBB
Music by JOHN KANDER

WILLKOMMEN
from the Musical CABARET

Words by FRED EBB
Music by JOHN KANDER

With spirit

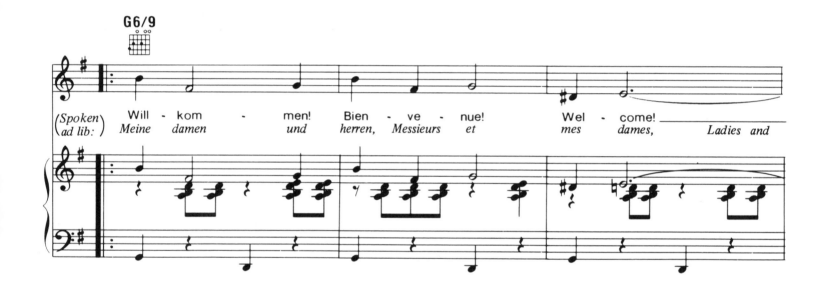

(Spoken) Will - kom - men! Bien - ve - nue! Wel - come! ___
(ad lib:) *Meine damen und herren, Messieurs et mes dames,* Ladies and

gentlemen,
Frem - der, E - tran - ger,
Guten abend, Bon soir,

NOWADAYS
from CHICAGO

Words by FRED EBB
Music by JOHN KANDER

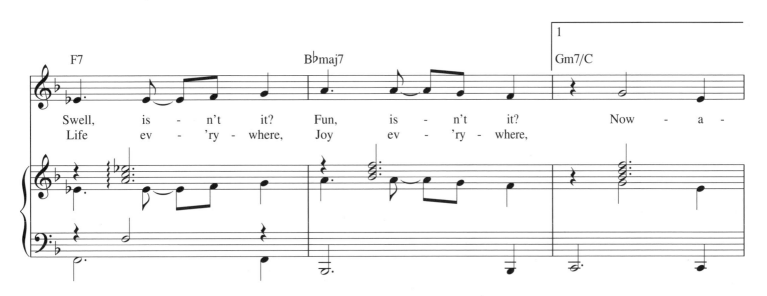

AND ALL THAT JAZZ

from CHICAGO

Words by FRED EBB
Music by JOHN KANDER

ROXIE
from CHICAGO

Words by FRED EBB
Music by JOHN KANDER

1. The name on ev-'ry-bod-y's lips is gon-na be Rox-ie,
2. They're gon-na wait out-side in line to get__ to see Rox-ie,

The la-dy rak-in' in the chips is gon-na be Rox-ie.
Think of those au-to-graphs I'll sign: "Good luck__ to you, Rox-ie."

I'm gon-na be a ce-leb-ri-ty, that means some-bod-y ev-'ry-one knows.
And I'll ap-pear in a lav-a-liere that goes all the way down__ to my waist.

LET IT GO

from THE FULL MONTY

Words and Music by
DAVID YAZBEK

LIFE WITH HAROLD

from THE FULL MONTY

Words and Music by
DAVID YAZBEK

93

cute in a suit and he loves me to boot. I'm tell-ing you, —

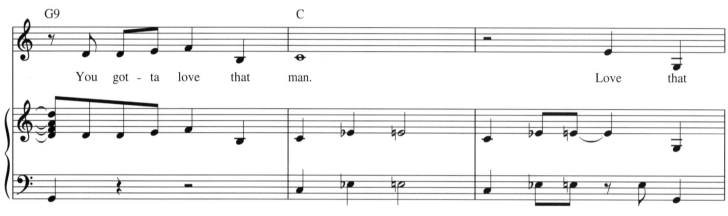

You got-ta love that man. Love that

man. I love that man.

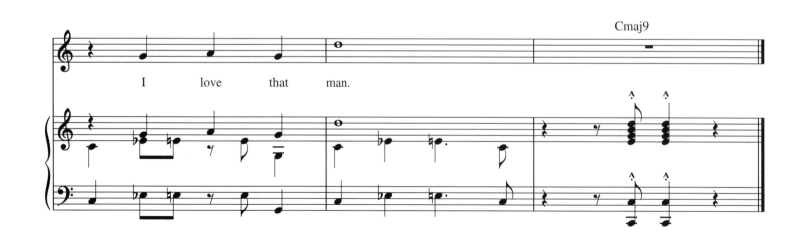

I love that man.

MAN
from THE FULL MONTY

Words and Music by
DAVID YAZBEK

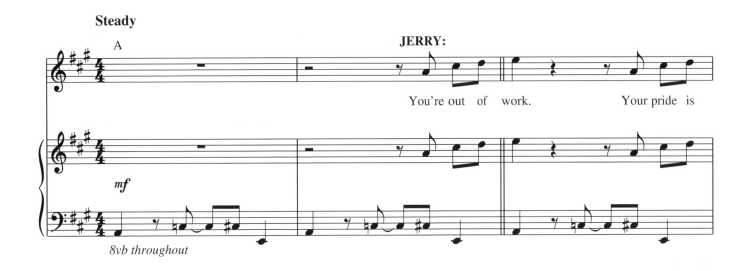

EVERYTHING'S COMING UP ROSES

from GYPSY

Words by STEPHEN SONDHEIM
Music by JULE STYNE

YOU'LL NEVER GET AWAY FROM ME

from GYPSY

Words by STEPHEN SONDHEIM
Music by JULE STYNE

Moderately, in 2

SMALL WORLD

from GYPSY

Words by STEPHEN SONDHEIM
Music by JULE STYNE

Moderately

Fun- ny, ___ you're a strang- er who's come here, come from an- oth- er town. Fun- ny, ___ I'm a strang- er my- self here. Small world, is- n't it?

I CAN HEAR THE BELLS

from HAIRSPRAY

Music by MARC SHAIMAN
Lyrics by MARC SHAIMAN and SCOTT WITTMAN

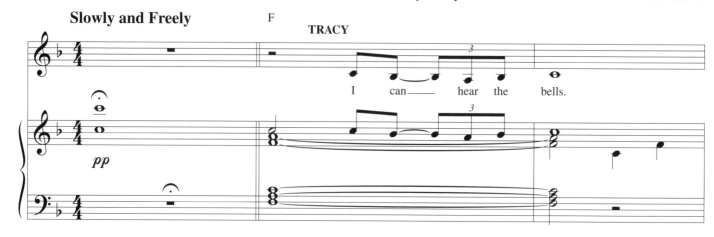

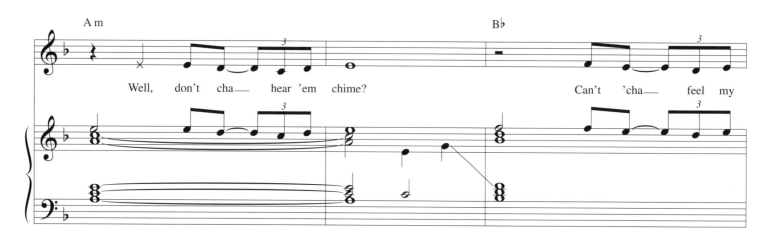

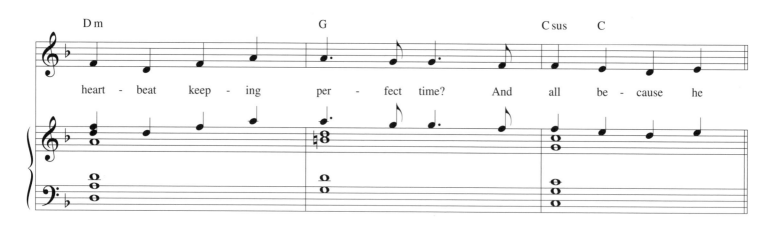

MAMA, I'M A BIG GIRL NOW

from HAIRSPRAY

Music by MARC SHAIMAN
Lyrics by MARC SHAIMAN and SCOTT WITTMAN

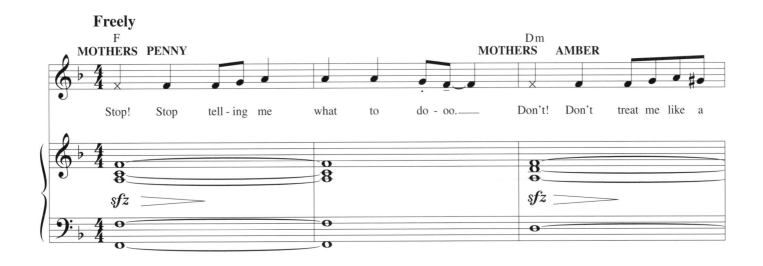

WELCOME TO THE 60's
from HAIRSPRAY

Music by MARC SHAIMAN
Lyrics by MARC SHAIMAN and SCOTT WITTMAN

THE MORNING REPORT

Disney Presents THE LION KING: THE BROADWAY MUSICAL

Music by ELTON JOHN
Lyrics by TIM RICE

Freely and leisurely

It's an hon-or and a priv-'lege, a du-ty I per-form with due sense of de-cor-um and with pride

With def-er-ence and great re-spect ver-y much the norm, plus a hint of syc-o-phan-cy on the side.

To lay be-fore my ru-ler all the facts a-bout his realm, to fill him in with all the beast-ly

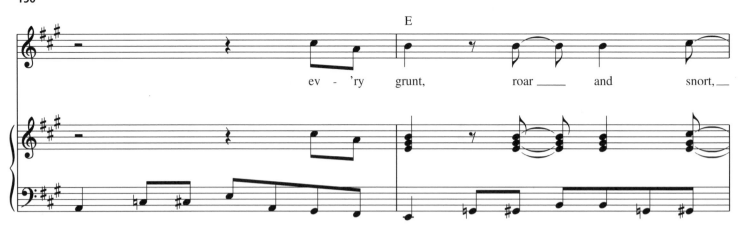

ev - 'ry grunt, roar ____ and snort, ____

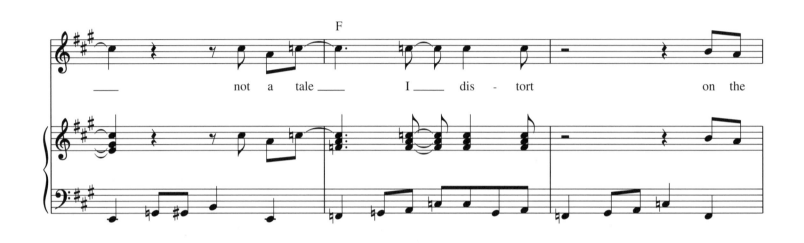

____ not a tale ____ I ____ dis - tort on the

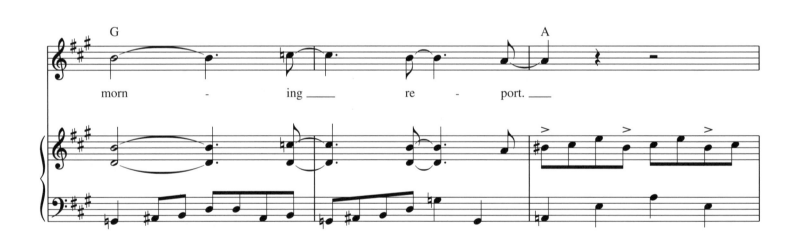

morn - ing ____ re - port. ____

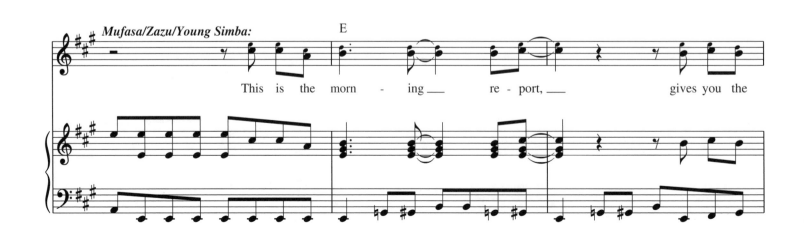

Mufasa/Zazu/Young Simba:

This is the morn - ing ____ re - port, ____ gives you the

long and the short, ev-'ry grunt, roar and snort,

not a tale I dis-tort on the

morn - ing re - port.

THEY LIVE IN YOU

Disney Presents THE LION KING: THE BROADWAY MUSICAL

Music and Lyrics by MARK MANCINA,
JAY RIFKIN and LEBO M

Spiritually, steadily

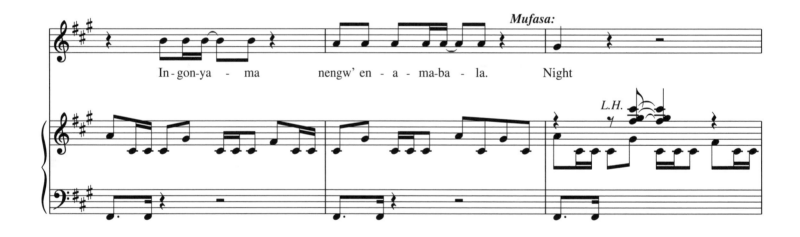

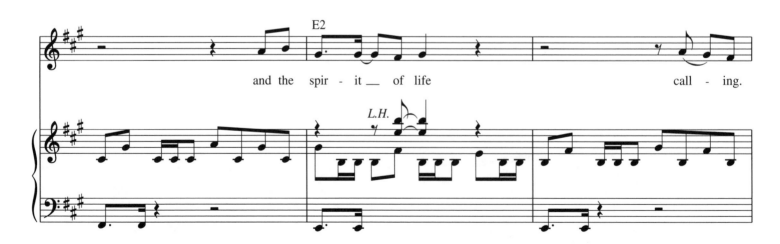

Can You Feel The Love Tonight

Disney Presents THE LION KING: THE BROADWAY MUSICAL

Music by ELTON JOHN
Lyrics by TIM RICE

DULCINEA

from MAN OF LA MANCHA

Music by MITCH LEIGH
Lyric by JOE DARION

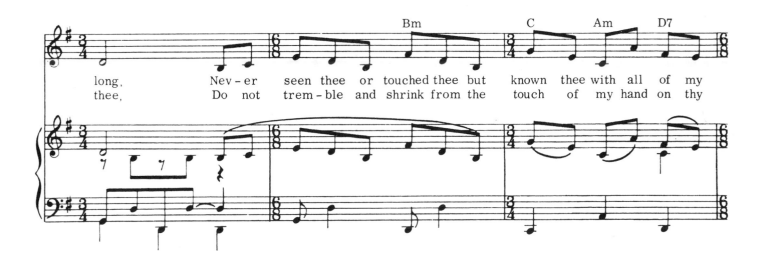

THE IMPOSSIBLE DREAM
(The Quest)
from MAN OF LA MANCHA

Lyric by JOE DARION
Music by MITCH LEIGH

Tempo di Bolero

THE LONGEST TIME
from MOVIN' OUT

Words and Music by
BILLY JOEL

Bright Rock and Roll

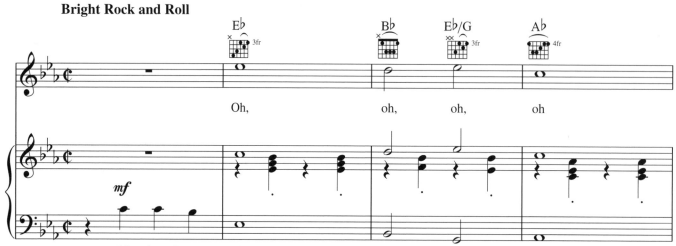

Oh, oh, oh, oh

l.h. played an octave lower throughout

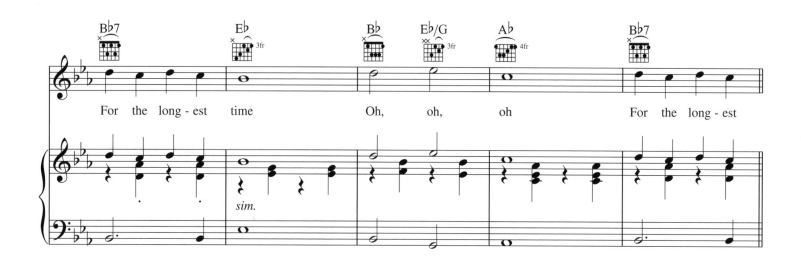

For the long-est time   Oh, oh, oh   For the long-est

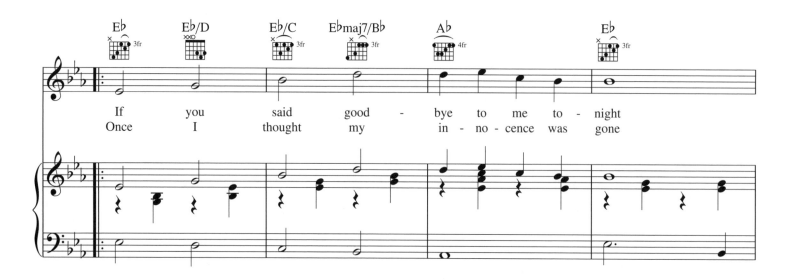

If you said good - bye to me to - night
Once I thought my in - no - cence was gone

MOVIN' OUT
(Anthony's Song)
from MOVIN' OUT

Words and Music by
BILLY JOEL

Moderately

Oo   Ah___   Ha -

Mm_____

An - tho - ny works___ in the gro - cer - y store___

Ser - geant O' - Lear - y is walk - in' the beat___   At

SHE'S GOT A WAY

from MOVIN' OUT

Words and Music by
BILLY JOEL

Slow and steady

She's got a way____ a-bout____
She's got a smile____ that heals____

____ her.   I don't know____ what it is,____ but I
____ me.   I don't know____ why it is,____ but I

know that I____ can't live with-out____ her.   She's got a way____ of
have to laugh____ when she re-veals____ me.   She's got a way____ of

SIMPLE
from NINE

Words and Music by
MAURY YESTON

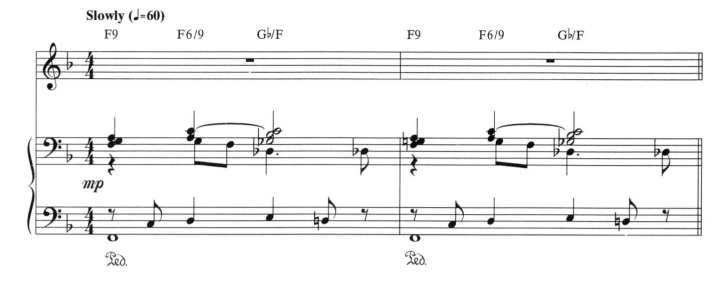

UNUSUAL WAY
(In a Very Unusual Way)
from NINE

Words and Music by
MAURY YESTON

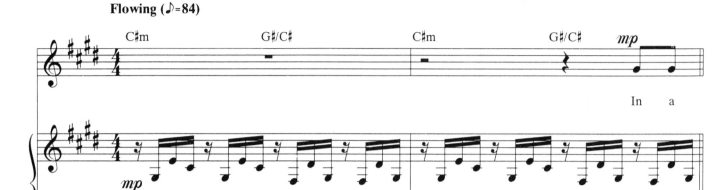

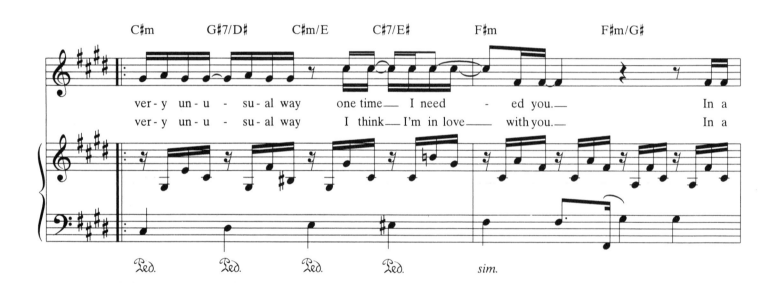

ALONG CAME BIALY

from THE PRODUCERS

Music and Lyrics by
MEL BROOKS

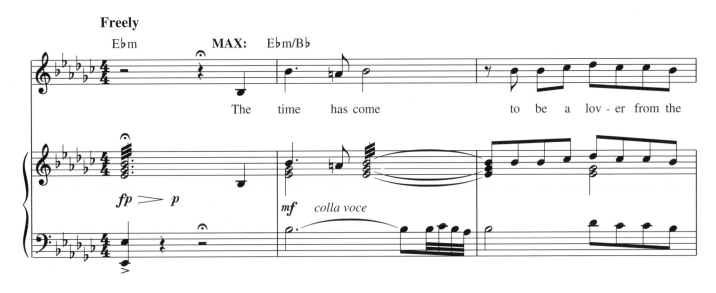

Freely

The time has come to be a lov-er from the

Ar - gen-tine, to slick my hair down with Bril - lian-tine,

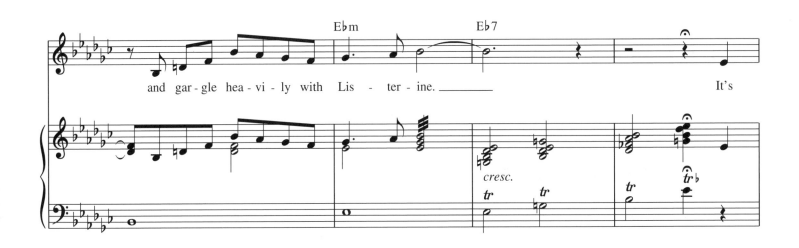

and gar-gle hea-vi-ly with Lis - ter-ine. _____ It's

HABEN SIE GEHÖRT DAS DEUTSCHE BAND?

(Have You Ever Heard the German Band?)

from THE PRODUCERS

Music and Lyrics by
MEL BROOKS

zetz mit a zap mit a zing! _____

Po - lish pol - kas, they're stu - pid und they're rot - ten! It

don't mean a thing if it ain't got that Schwei - gen Rei - gen

schö - nen Schüt - zen Schmüt - zen Sau - er - bra - ten. *Key change!* Ve're say - in'

(spoken:)

I WANNA BE A PRODUCER

from THE PRODUCERS

Music and Lyrics by
MEL BROOKS

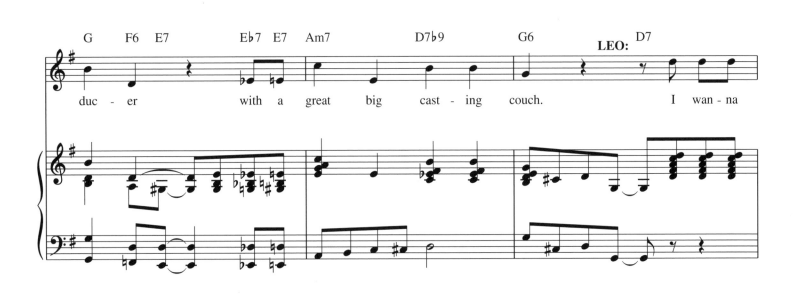

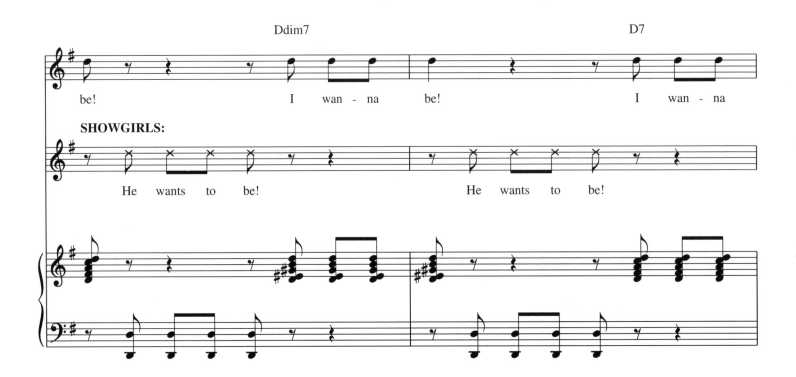

Straight 8ths
Swing!
D7 C#dim7/D D7 C#dim7/D Am/D Bm/D Am/D D
Ab6
be the great-est, gran-dest and most fa - bu - lous pro - duc - er in the world!
He wants to be a pro -
Straight 8ths
ff
rall.
Bb7
Bb13
LEO:
I
duc - er he's got - ta dine with a duch - ess and a duke
Bbm
Bbm7
Eb7 Bb7b9 Bbm7/Eb
just got - ta be a pro - duc - er, drink cham - pagne un - til I puke.

LEO:
Ab6 · A9b5 · Ab · Ab/G · Ab/Gb · F7

— I wan - na be a pro - duc - er show the

SHOWGIRLS:

Drink cham-pagne till he pukes!

LEO:
F7 · Eb/G F7/A · Bbm6 · Bbm · Dbm(#7) · Dbm6

world just what I've got I'm gon-na put-on shows _ that will en - thrall _ 'em

gliss.

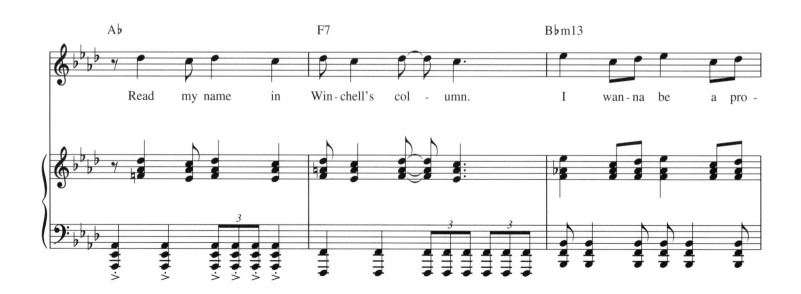

Ab · F7 · Bbm13

Read my name in Win-chell's col - umn. I wan-na be a pro -

ONE SONG GLORY
from RENT

Words and Music by
JONATHAN LARSON

TAKE ME OR LEAVE ME

from RENT

Words and Music by
JONATHAN LARSON

FORGET ABOUT THE BOY

from THOROUGHLY MODERN MILLIE

Music by JEANINE TESORI
Lyrics by DICK SCANLAN

HOW THE OTHER HALF LIVES

from THOROUGHLY MODERN MILLIE

Music by JEANINE TESORI
Lyrics by DICK SCANLAN

Moderately, in 2; dramatically

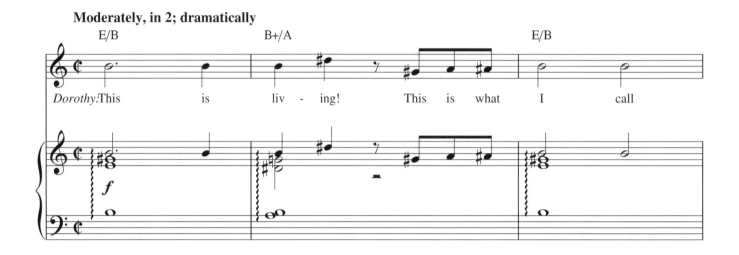

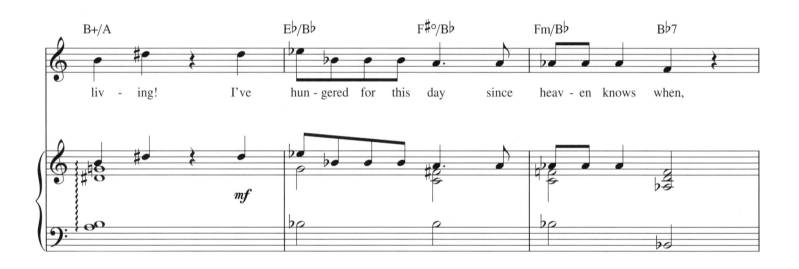

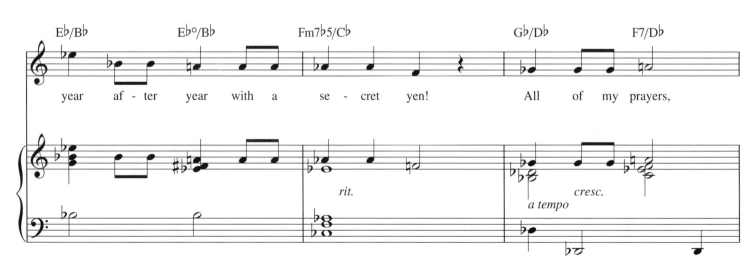

THOROUGHLY MODERN MILLIE

from THOROUGHLY MODERN MILLIE

Words by SAMMY CAHN
Music by JAMES VAN HEUSEN

Sod - om and__ Go - mor - rah - ble!__ But the fact is,

ev - 'ry - thing to - day is thor - ough - ly mod - ern.

(Bands are get - tin' jazz - i - er.) Ev - 'ry - thing to - day is start - ing to

go. (Cars are get - tin' snaz - zi - er.) Men say

SEASONS OF LOVE
from RENT

Words and Music by
JONATHAN LARSON